INVESTIGATING THE UNEXPLAINED

BIGFOOT

BY EMILY ROSE OACHS

BELLWETHER MEDIA • MINNEAPOLIS, MN

Blastoff! Discovery launches
a new mission: reading to learn.
Filled with facts and features, each
book offers you an exciting new
world to explore!

This edition first published in 2019 by Bellwether Media, Inc.

No part of this publication may be reproduced in whole or in
part without written permission of the publisher.
For information regarding permission, write to
Bellwether Media, Inc., Attention: Permissions Department,
6012 Blue Circle Drive, Minnetonka, MN 55343.

Library of Congress Cataloging-in-Publication Data

Names: Oachs, Emily Rose, author.
Title: Bigfoot / by Emily Rose Oachs.
Description: Minneapolis, MN : Bellwether Media, Inc., 2019. |
    Series: Blastoff! Discovery: Investigating the Unexplained |
    Includes bibliographical references and index.
Identifiers: LCCN 2018003683 (print) | LCCN 2018015803
    (ebook) | ISBN 9781626178526 (hardcover : alk. paper)|
    ISBN 9781681035932 (ebook)
Subjects: LCSH: Sasquatch–Juvenile literature.
Classification: LCC QL89.2.S2 (ebook) | LCC QL89.2.S2 O23
    2019 (print) | DDC 001.944–dc23

LC record available at https://lccn.loc.gov/2018003683

Editor: Paige Polinsky   Designer: Andrea Schneider

Printed in the United States of America, North Mankato, MN.

TABLE OF CONTENTS

MYSTERY IN THE NIGHT

Maribel and Robert hike deep into the wilderness. They are far from any cities or roads. The pair finds a clearing in the thick forest and sets up camp. They keep their cameras close at hand. Bigfoot could appear at any moment!

As night falls, the investigators pull gear from their packs. Robert's night-vision goggles are at the ready. Maribel flips the switch to turn on her audio recorder. Then they wait. Minutes tick by slowly, and Maribel begins to doze off.

REC

5

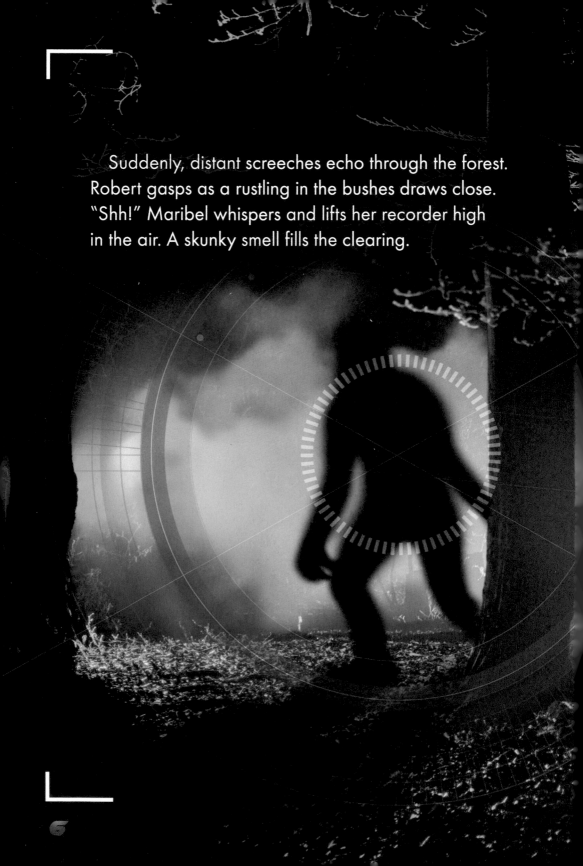

Suddenly, distant screeches echo through the forest. Robert gasps as a rustling in the bushes draws close. "Shh!" Maribel whispers and lifts her recorder high in the air. A skunky smell fills the clearing.

REC

WHAT'S IN A NAME?

Bigfoot is also called Sasquatch. This
name comes from the word "Sasq'ets." In
the Native American language Halkomelem,
this means "hairy man"!

Robert peers into the darkness through his goggles.
Maribel scrambles for the camera. A large shadow
moves among the trees and disappears into the night.
In the morning, the Bigfoot hunters search the area.
Maribel snaps photos of a large footprint on the soft
ground. Was Bigfoot here?

SECRETS OF THE FOREST

Some people believe that a large primate roams North America's thick, distant forests. They call this mysterious cryptid Bigfoot, or Sasquatch. Native American stories of Bigfoot go back hundreds of years. Many of these tales describe Bigfoot as peaceful.

Most researchers believe that Bigfoot is not one creature but a species. The creatures are said to walk upright on two legs and have humanlike faces. But witnesses claim they are much taller and heavier than humans. Hair covers much of their bodies. Many early reports of Bigfoot came from the Pacific Northwest. But sightings have been reported across the United States and Canada!

BIGFOOT SIGHTINGS IN U.S. AND CANADA

3,313 reports from 1921 to 2013

Canada

United States

light report levels
moderate report levels
heavy report levels

ONE BIG MYSTERY

In 1811, British explorer David Thompson found strange tracks in the Canadian Rockies. He described them in his journal. Some people believe this is the earliest record of Bigfoot footprints. More Bigfoot stories arrived in the late 1800s and onward. One man even claimed a Bigfoot family kidnapped him!

The Bigfoot mystery struck Northern California in 1958. There, a construction worker found large footprints around his tractor. A newspaper named the footprints' creator "Bigfoot." Many years later, the worker's children claimed that the prints had been faked. Still, many believe the tracks were real.

BIG FEET, BIG BODY

AVERAGE AMERICAN MALE

BIGFOOT

People believe Bigfoot can reach 10 feet (3 meters) in height and 1,000 pounds (454 kilograms) in weight. Its feet may be 16 inches (41 centimeters) long!

REC

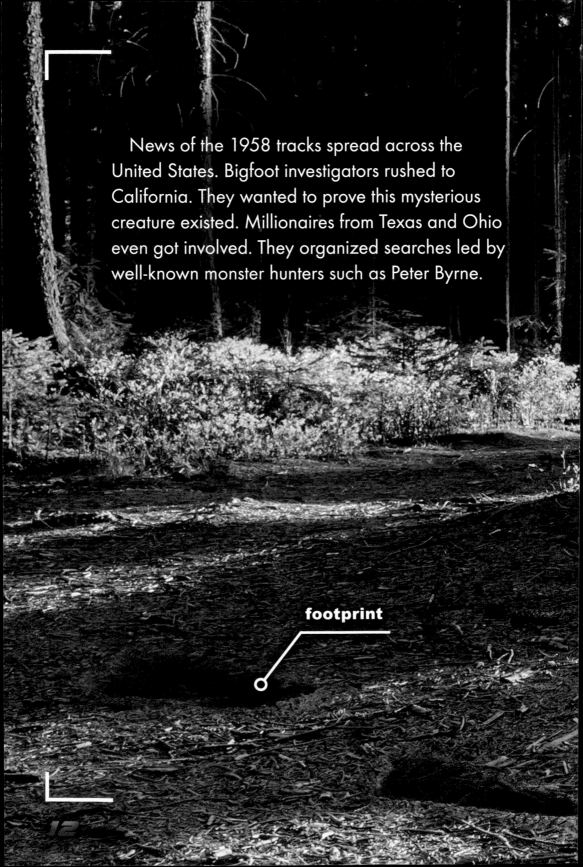

News of the 1958 tracks spread across the United States. Bigfoot investigators rushed to California. They wanted to prove this mysterious creature existed. Millionaires from Texas and Ohio even got involved. They organized searches led by well-known monster hunters such as Peter Byrne.

footprint

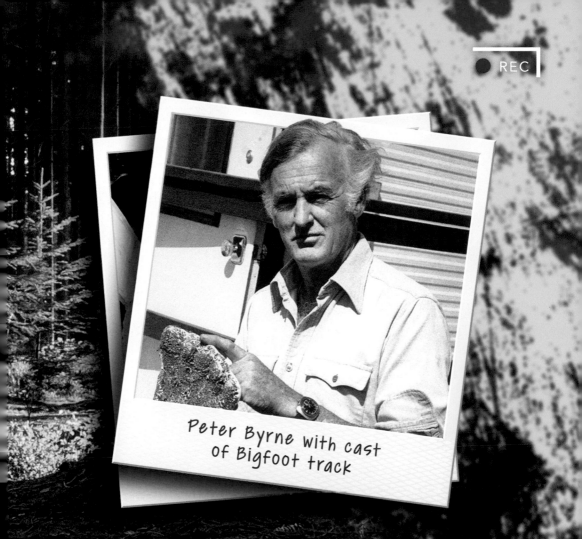

Peter Byrne with cast
of Bigfoot track

Investigators brought cameras, hoping for photos and videos of Bigfoot. They kept plaster on hand to create casts of tracks. With camping gear, investigators could spend weeks in Bigfoot's forest home. By the 1990s, off-road vehicles allowed them to travel through thick forests in search of the creature.

SIERRA SOUNDS

In the 1970s, two Bigfoot researchers recorded strange noises in California's Sierra Nevada Mountains. They claimed their tape contained 90 minutes of Bigfoot chatter. Some experts say the Sierra Sounds are proof of Bigfoot using language!

In 1967, two investigators claimed they filmed Bigfoot in California. The grainy video became famous! Two years later, a trail of 1,089 tracks appeared in snowy northern Washington. The detailed prints seemed to reveal a deformed right foot. Sightings continued to pop up around North America.

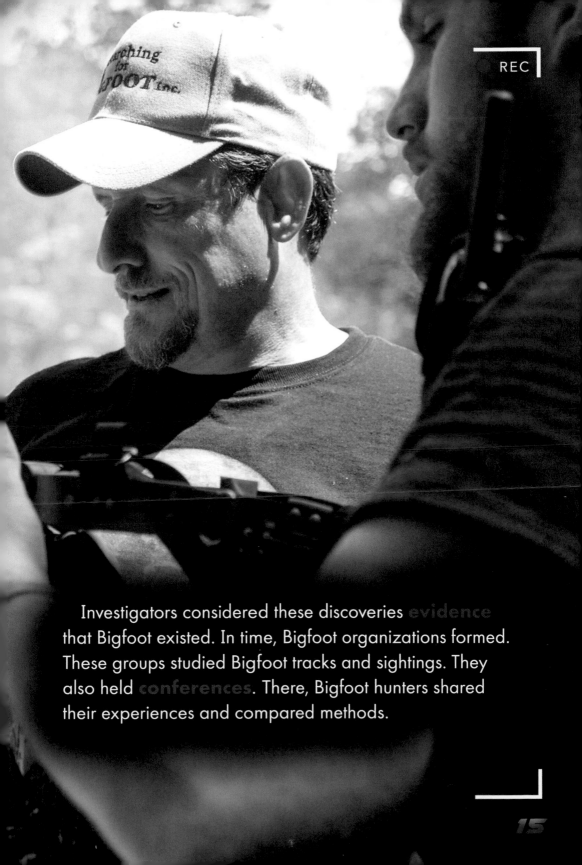

Investigators considered these discoveries evidence that Bigfoot existed. In time, Bigfoot organizations formed. These groups studied Bigfoot tracks and sightings. They also held conferences. There, Bigfoot hunters shared their experiences and compared methods.

Roger Patterson and Bob Gimlin

PROFILE: THE PATTERSON-GIMLIN FILM

In the fall of 1967, Roger Patterson and Bob Gimlin set out for the thick wilderness of northern California. Stories of Bigfoot encounters drew them there to film a **documentary**. On October 20, Patterson and Gimlin spotted a hairy creature walking across a clearing. In one minute, it was gone. But Patterson had captured it on film!

Hollywood costumers, **special effects** experts, and scientists have studied the video. Some claim it is a **hoax**, but that has never been proven.

creature filmed by
Patterson and Gimlin

BIGFOOT CAPITAL

Willow Creek, California, is known as the
"Bigfoot Capital of the World." The town is a
few miles from where the Patterson-Gimlin film
was shot. Each September, its Bigfoot Days
festival celebrates the mystery of Bigfoot!

SEARCHING FOR BIGFOOT

Modern investigators pack a mix of old and new gear. Notebooks are still key for logging Bigfoot encounters. Plaster remains another major tool. Casts allow Bigfoot hunters to study prints at home. They can compare them to other tracks and study them for anatomical details.

DARTING AROUND

Some investigators carry dart guns. If they spot Bigfoot, they can shoot it with a dart. The dart collects blood from Bigfoot without harming the creature!

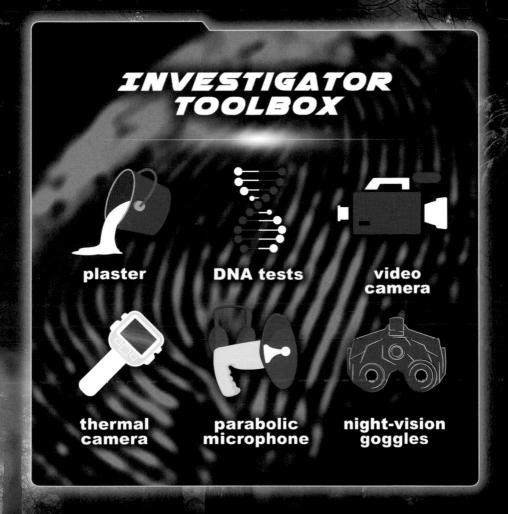

INVESTIGATOR TOOLBOX

plaster

DNA tests

video camera

thermal camera

parabolic microphone

night-vision goggles

Investigators often use small plastic bags to store possible Bigfoot evidence, such as hair or blood. Scientists test this for DNA. If a sample does not match any known DNA, it might be from Bigfoot!

trail camera

No Bigfoot kit is complete without cameras. Investigators need video and still cameras to record any live encounters. But cameras are also handy when researchers find footprints, droppings, or other Bigfoot evidence. They take photos so they can closely examine this evidence later.

Modern cameras capture high-quality photos and videos. They can take hundreds of photos at a time. Some investigators also hide trail cameras deep in the forest. These cameras start recording when they sense movement nearby.

body heat
illustration

Investigators believe that Bigfoot is most active
at night. Night-vision goggles allow investigators
to see in the dark. Thermal cameras pick up body
heat from nearby animals. They then show that heat
on screen. This helps investigators record creatures
lurking in the forest.

Investigators do not just look for Bigfoot. They
listen, too. Bigfoot is said to knock on trees, howl, and
whistle. Parabolic microphones let investigators
capture these sounds from far away. Some researchers
even try to copy those noises to attract Bigfoot.
They use their own voices as tools!

HOW THERMAL CAMERAS WORK

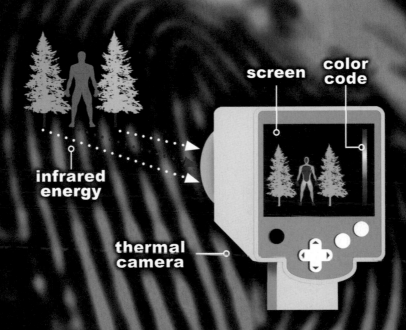

screen   color code

infrared energy

thermal camera

1. **All objects give off heat. This heat takes the form of light waves called infrared energy.**

2. **The human eye cannot see this energy. But a thermal camera senses it.**

3. **The camera uses a color code. It gives each temperature a different shade.**

4. **An animal's body is often warmer than its surroundings. It stands out on the screen!**

SASQUATCH SKEPTICS

Most scientists are not convinced that Bigfoot is real. They question how such a large animal could stay hidden for so long. They also point out that nobody has dug up Bigfoot bones or teeth. How could evidence of a giant primate be missing from the North American fossil record?

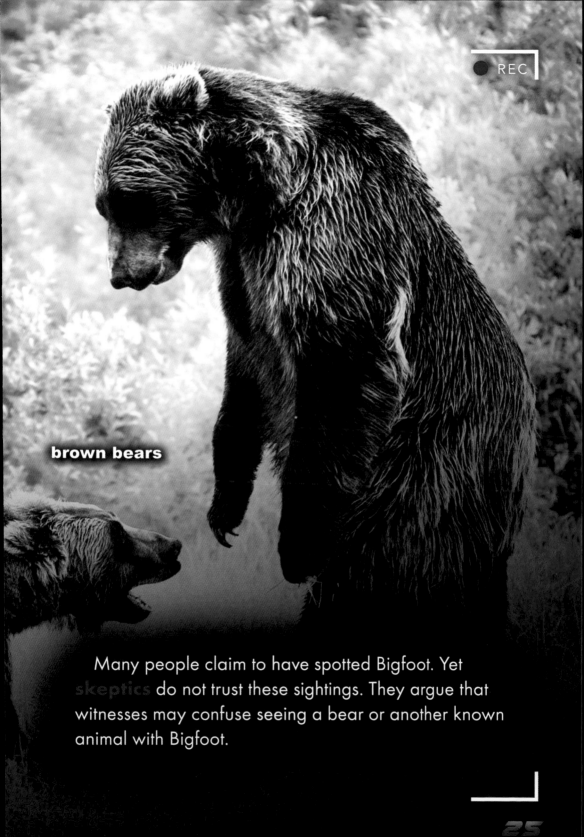

brown bears

Many people claim to have spotted Bigfoot. Yet skeptics do not trust these sightings. They argue that witnesses may confuse seeing a bear or another known animal with Bigfoot.

FOOL ME ONCE...

In 2008, Rick Dyer fooled many into
believing he had found a dead Bigfoot.
The body turned out to be a Halloween
costume. Four years later, Dyer charged
people money to see a different fake!

Skeptics also believe that people have faked evidence
of Bigfoot to earn money and fame. They point out that
Bigfoot tracks come in different sizes and shapes. People
could easily create phony Bigfoot feet to make fake tracks.
They could also fake Bigfoot noises.

Even images of Bigfoot do not sway skeptics. They point out that photos and video of Bigfoot are often blurry. Experts can often identify when a person is in costume. Sometimes evidence is digitally altered.

BIGFOOT BELIEVERS

There have been thousands of Bigfoot sightings. Many people have also found footprints, hair, and other evidence of Bigfoot. Still, nobody has been able to prove these creatures exist.

Even so, the mystery of Bigfoot continues to fascinate people. Websites and television shows are dedicated to finding the creature. More investigators and rapidly improving technology mean that discovering Bigfoot is becoming more likely. If Bigfoot exists, it may not be long before the truth comes out.

BIGFOOT PLAYS BASKETBALL

Bigfoot has even been seen in the NBA! In 1993, Seattle's former team, the SuperSonics, introduced Squatch the Bigfoot as its mascot.

GLOSSARY

anatomical—relating to the makeup of the body

audio recorder—a device that captures and saves sounds

casts—molds of something's shape

conferences—large meetings of people to talk about shared work or interests, usually over several days

cryptid—an animal that may or may not exist

deformed—not having a normal shape, especially because of a problem in the way something has grown

DNA—a tiny substance that carries information about the makeup of a living thing

documentary—a movie or TV show that tells the facts about real topics

evidence—information that helps prove or disprove something

fossil record—the fossils, or remains, that have been discovered in a place

hoax—an act meant to fool or trick someone

investigators—people who try to find out the facts about something in order to learn if or how it happened

night-vision goggles—eyewear that magnifies light coming in to allow people to see in the dark

Pacific Northwest—a region in the northwestern United States along the coast of the Pacific Ocean; the Pacific Northwest includes Washington, Oregon, and parts of Idaho and Montana.

parabolic microphones—microphones surrounded by a curved dish; the dish helps collect sound from a distance.

plaster—wet matter that hardens when it becomes dry

primate—an intelligent mammal with hands and feet; humans, apes, and monkeys are all primates.

skeptics—people who doubt something is true

special effects—tricks that make fake things seem real, often used in movies

species—a group of animals or plants that are similar

thermal cameras—cameras that can pick up on and show heat

TO LEARN MORE

AT THE LIBRARY

Colson, Mary. *Bigfoot and Yeti: Myth or Reality?* North Mankato, Minn.: Capstone Press, 2019.

Noll, Elizabeth. *Bigfoot.* Mankato, Minn.: Black Rabbit Books, 2017.

Peabody, Erin. *Bigfoot.* New York, N.Y.: Little Bee, 2017.

ON THE WEB

Learning more about Bigfoot is as easy as 1, 2, 3.

1. Go to www.factsurfer.com.

2. Enter "Bigfoot" into the search box.

3. Click the "Surf" button and you will see a list of related web sites.

With factsurfer.com, finding more information is just a click away.

INDEX

NOV - - 2018